POWER-FILLED!

Leading Children into the Baptism into the Holy Spirit

DECADE OF PENTECOST EDITION

Philip Malcolm
and Robin Malcolm

Including

A Lesson Plan for Teaching Children about the Baptism in the Holy Spirit

All Scripture quotations taken from the HOLY BIBLE, NEW INTERNATIONAL VERSION ®. Copyright ©1973, 1978, 1984 by International Bible Society.

Malcolm, Philip and Malcolm, Robin
Power-Filled: Leading Children into the Baptism in the Holy Spirit / Malcolm and Malcolm

1. Biblical Studies. 2. Theology. 3. Pentecostal. 4. Children's Ministries. 5. Holy Spirit. 6. Baptism in the Holy Spirit

This book is a reprint of the original book by Philip and Robin Malcolm entitled, *Power-Filled: Leading Children into the Baptism in the Holy Spirit* published by the authors in 2008. It is being republished in this Decade of Pentecost Edition with the authors' permission.

ISBN: 978-0-9903008-1-6

Printed in the United States of America
Published by AIA Publications, Springfield, MO, USA
A Decade of Pentecost Publication

TABLE OF CONTENTS

Part 1: Teacher's Manual

**Part 2: Lesson Plan for Teaching Children about
the Baptism in the Holy Spirit**

Preface to the
Decade of Pentecost Edition

Thank God for His amazing promise to pour out His Spirit on all flesh--even on our "sons and daughters" (Acts 2:17-18). This is why we at the Acts in Africa Initiative are so happy to present to you this valuable resource, *Power Filled: Leading Children into the Baptism in the Holy Spirit,* written by veteran missionaries and children's ministers Philip and Robin Malcolm. It is a reprint of their book by the same title published by the Africa's Children "Children's Ministry Toolbox."

We are republishing this book on the occasion of the launching of the Africa Assemblies of God "Decade of Pentecost" 2015 emphasis, "Passing Pentecost to the Next Generation." The theme is based on the psalmist's declaration, "I will declare your power to the next generation" (Psalm 71:18). The Decade of Pentecost from 2010 to 2020 is a cooperative ten-year, Spirit-empowered missionary emphasis of the fifty national Assemblies of God churches in sub-Sahara Africa and the Indian Ocean Basin.

The cornerstone of the emphasis is the shared goal of seeing ten million new believers baptized in the Holy Spirit and then mobilized as Spirit-empowered witnesses to the lost. It is expected that, as a result of this emphasis, millions of people will come to know Christ as Savior, thousands of new churches will be planted, hundreds of new indigenous African missionaries will be deployed, and many of the yet-to-be-reached tribes of sub-Sahara will be reached with the life-changing gospel of Christ.

We further expect that during the decade a significant percentage of those who are baptized in the Holy Spirit will be children. At present there is an estimated five million children and youth up to age 15 attending in AG churches in sub-Saharan Africa. A powerful outpouring of the Spirit on these millions of children and young people could plant the seeds of a spiritual revolution in the church. This outcome would ensure a bright future for the African church—and potentially for all of Africa.

With these things in mind I commend this book to you. I hope that you will use the insights and practical suggestions found herein to lead many children into the wonderful Pentecostal experience. And I trust that you will train the and mobilize them to reach other children, and even adults, with the gospel.

Dr. Denzil R. Miller
Director
Acts in Africa Initiative

INTRODUCTION

The year 2006 marked the 100th anniversary of the Pentecostal movement that gave birth to the Assemblies of God. This manual is an attempt to share the basis of our Pentecostal heritage with our children. We believe that every Christian needs the power of the Holy Spirit functioning in their lives.

This manual is merely an introduction to life in the Spirit. It is not meant to be a comprehensive course on the Holy Spirit. In fact, the material focuses primarily on one key aspect—the baptism in the Holy Spirit. Our hope is that this manual will be the starting point which allows the Holy Spirit to become a central theme in your ministry and in the lives of your children.

The material that follows is presented as a series of questions and answers. Each chapter looks briefly at one aspect of the baptism in the Holy Spirit. As you begin reading this manual, take time to carefully read Acts 1:3-9 and Acts chapter 2. The detailed account of the disciples on the day of Pentecost forms the foundation of our study. For more information on this topic and the Holy Spirit in general, a list of resources is included, which you can use for further study.

We pray that God blesses your ministry as you reach out to children. May the Holy Spirit give you the power to change your world for His glory.

PART 1:
TEACHER'S MANUAL

CHAPTER 1

WHO IS THE HOLY SPIRIT
AND
WHAT DOES HE DO?

To lead your students into this precious gift of the baptism in the Holy Spirit, you must begin with an understanding of who the Holy Spirit is and what He does.

Imagine a school teacher who did not understand basic mathematics. She could not teach it to her students. If she tried, the students would just be confused. In the same way, if you, as a spiritual teacher, do not understand the Holy Spirit, who He is and how He works in your life and the lives of your students, your instruction will only confuse your students.

Who is the Holy Spirit?

The Holy Spirit is God. This fact is central to understanding the Holy Spirit. We believe in one true God who shows Himself to us in the Trinity. The Trinity is one God expressed in three persons; God the Father, God the Son, and God the Holy Spirit.

All three exist at once and share all the characteristics and power of God. Yet each is, at the same time, a separate person. Completely understanding the Trinity is beyond our human minds. As Christians, we accept by faith that certain aspects of God are beyond our understanding. For the purpose of this discussion, it is only important that we understand that the Holy Spirit is God.

Jesus referred to the Holy Spirit as God in Matthew 28:19 when He told His disciples to go and make disciples by baptizing them in the name of the Father and of the Son and of the Holy Spirit. The writers of the Bible also refer to the Holy Spirit in this same manner. 2 Corinthians 13:14 and 1 Peter 1:2 both specifically list all three persons of the Godhead, including the Holy Spirit.

In the book of Acts, Jesus' disciples frequently talked about the Holy Spirit as having the characteristics of God and doing the work of God. For further study, read Acts 1:16; 5:3,9,32; 7:51; 8:29,39; 10:19; 11:12; 13:2,4; 15:28; 16:6,7; 20:23,28; 28:25.

What Does the Holy Spirit Do?

Because He is God, the Holy Spirit does the work of God. Genesis 1:1,2 specifically states that the Spirit was present when the world was created. He is God from the beginning, and He is active throughout the Bible.

The Holy Spirit does many different things. Some of them, such as inspiring scripture and commanding and calling believers, are tasks that are shared with the other persons of the Trinity. Other tasks are uniquely works of the Holy Spirit.

The Holy Spirit influences a person's life at the time of their salvation. It is the Holy Spirit who sanctifies, or cleans, our hearts when we ask God to forgive our sins (2 Thessalonians 2:13). After we become believers, the Holy Spirit becomes a voice of conscience. He speaks into our hearts and tells us when we have disobeyed God

(John 16:8). He leads us to the truth (John 16:13-15) and comforts us in times of sorrow (John 14:16, 26).

A Spirit-filled believer has the help of the Holy Spirit to pray as God wants. Because we do not know everything, we sometimes do not know how to pray. But the Holy Spirit knows everything. He prays through us when we speak in tongues—our heavenly language. Romans 8:26-27 says that He speaks for us.

The Holy Spirit does many other things for us as believers. In this manual about the baptism in the Holy Spirit, we will focus on one important thing the Holy Spirit does in our lives: He gives us power to witness to others.

The first two chapters of Acts describe in detail how the disciples were given the gift of the Holy Spirit on the day of Pentecost. The gift immediately became evident as Peter, who had previously denied even knowing Jesus, boldly preached to the worshippers in the temple. The Holy Spirit can give us power and boldness to tell others about Jesus!

Everyone who accepts God's gift of salvation receives the Holy Spirit into his life, because the Holy Spirit is God. But the Bible clearly shows us that this power from the Holy Spirit, referred to as the "baptism in the Holy Spirit" is given to us as a separate gift, different from the gift of salvation.

The disciples, who had already chosen to follow Jesus more than three years earlier, were filled with the Holy Spirit on the day of Pentecost (Acts 2:4) and began to witness boldly. Later in the New Testament, there are more examples of the gift of the Holy Spirit being different from the gift of salvation. In Acts 19:1-7, Paul asked the disciples at Ephesus (Note: They were already believers) if they had received the Holy Spirit when they believed. When they responded that they had not, he prayed for them and "the Holy Spirit came on them, and they spoke in tongues and prophesied" (Acts 19:6 NIV).

The Assemblies of God is committed to the baptism in the Holy Spirit because the experience is an important focus of New Testament Christianity. It is so important, in fact, that it forms one of the four core beliefs of our fellowship.[1] However, our children will never have the Pentecostal experience unless we pass it on to them.

---

[1] The Baptism in the Holy Spirit is one of the "Four Defining Truths of the Assemblies of God." In a statement of the four core beliefs of the fellowship, the Assemblies of God states, "All believers are entitled to and should ardently expect and earnestly seek the promise of the Father, the baptism in the Holy Spirit and fire, according to the command of our Lord Jesus Christ. This was the normal experience of all in the early Christian Church. With it comes the enduement of power for life and service, the bestowment of the gifts and their uses in the work of the ministry."

CHAPTER 2

WHAT IS THE BAPTISM IN THE HOLY SPIRIT?

Before He returned to heaven, Jesus gave His disciples their final instructions. He told them to be His witnesses throughout the world. But before they could be His witnesses, He emphasized that they needed to receive the gift of the Holy Spirit. He referred to this gift as "the promise of the Father" (Acts 1:4 NIV), and assured them that the promised Spirit would be their source of power to accomplish their mission (Acts 1:8 NIV).

The Book of Acts is a marvelous record of the first century Church—a Church who was obedient to their Lord's command to receive the baptism in the Holy Spirit. As a result, they effectively spread the gospel of Jesus Christ throughout their known world. So what is this "baptism in the Holy Spirit" that allowed them to succeed?

What Do I Need to Know about the Baptism in the Holy Spirit?

In the previous chapter, we discussed some of the things that the Holy Spirit does for Christians. The Holy Spirit is active in every believer's life from the time of salvation. But it is important to remember that the baptism in the Holy Spirit is a separate work from what the Holy Spirit does at the time of salvation. These two events may sometimes happen together, or may be separated by days, months, or even years, depending on when the believer's heart is ready.

This work of the Holy Spirit which we call the "Baptism" is an infilling of spiritual power. This power is given to us for a specific reason: to fulfill the mission of God. It was for this purpose that Jesus told His disciples to wait in Jerusalem for the gift of the Holy Spirit: so they would have power to be witnesses and make disciples of all nations (Acts 1:8).

The baptism in the Holy Spirit is for anyone who has already received Jesus as their Lord and Savior. When the believers prayed on the Day of Pentecost, "All of them were filled with the Holy Spirit and began to speak in other tongues as the Spirit enabled them" (Acts 2:4 NIV). Nobody was left out. It was not just the apostles who were filled, but all the men and women in that group of 120 persons. The apostle Peter spoke to the onlookers and told them that after they repented and believed in Jesus, they would be filled. He said, "The promise is for you and your children and for all who are far off—for all whom the Lord our God will call" (Acts 2:39 NIV). The baptism in the Holy Spirit is promised to anyone who has already confessed faith in Jesus Christ and has become part of God's family.

The baptism in the Holy Spirit is the beginning of a Spirit-filled life. As a result of this gift of power in our lives, the Holy Spirit can help us live powerful Christian lives and conquer sin (Romans 8:4-5). He can help us grow in spiritual maturity and develop the "fruit of the Spirit." Characteristics such as love, joy and peace will grow in our lives at the same time as we grow in Spirit-filled ministry (See Galatians 5:22-25 for a complete list of the fruit of the Spirit.).

16

Finally, it is important to know that the baptism in the Holy Spirit is a gift from God. It is free. It is not earned. The only thing we must do is to ask for it. In Luke 11:13, Jesus promises that the Father will give the Holy Spirit to those who ask Him.

This does not mean that everyone who asks for this gift will receive it right away. God, in His wisdom, will baptize each believer when their hearts are right before Him. They will receive when they are ready to use the power and responsibility that comes with this gift. Even the disciples, when they received the gift on the day of Pentecost, had waited and prayed for days before they received.

How Do I Know If I've Received This Gift?

If all you have to do is ask God to baptize you in the Holy Spirit, how do you know when you have received this gift? You cannot see the Holy Spirit, so how do you know when He has filled you with His power?

Jesus compared the baptism in the Holy Spirit with water baptism (Acts 1:5). When a believer is baptized in water, he is immersed. When he comes out of the water, he feels the water on his skin and clothing. Others can see that he has been baptized, because he is wet!

The baptism in the Holy Spirit is a similar experience. You can feel it happen, just as you feel wet when you are baptized in water. However, it is more than a feeling; it is a real experience. Everyone who has been baptized in the Spirit knows without question when and where it happened. But more importantly, they also know who baptized them. For there is only one divine Baptizer—our Lord Jesus Christ! "He will baptize you with the Holy Spirit" (Mark 1:8 NIV).

God has also given us a visible sign that we have received His gift. The Bible calls this sign "speaking in other tongues." It is the first visible evidence of the baptism in the Holy Spirit. Speaking in tongues means that the person who is baptized begins to speak in a language that they do not know and have not learned. This language is sometimes called a prayer language or a heavenly language.

Five times the book of Acts tells of believers being baptized in the Spirit. Three of the passages give details about the event, and speaking in tongues is mentioned each time (Acts 2,10,19). In Acts chapter 10, speaking in tongues is specifically listed as proof of the baptism in the Holy Spirit.

The circumcised believers who had come with Peter were astonished that the gift of the Holy Spirit had been poured out, even on the Gentiles. For they heard them speaking in tongues (Acts 10:45-46).

Two other cases of believers being baptized in the Holy Spirit are given in the book of Acts, but the details are not supplied. However, in those cases, the writer of Acts strongly implies that speaking with other tongues accompanied the experience. In Acts chapter 8, Simon saw something that prompted him to offer money for the power to impart such a gift (most likely, speaking in tongues). In Acts chapter 9, Saul (who later became Paul) is filled with the Spirit without the mention of any details. However, Paul later testified, "I speak in tongues more than all of you" (1 Corinthians 14:18 NIV). Logically, we can conclude that he began speaking in tongues when he was baptized in the Holy Spirit. The Bible is clear, then, that speaking in tongues always accompanied the baptism in the Holy Spirit. It is, however, only the first evidence that a person has been filled, and it is not the goal or reason for the gift.

As previously stated, the baptism in the Holy Spirit is a filling with power. Using the power to witness, showing the fruit of the Spirit and praying powerfully are other evidences that a Christian has been filled with the Holy Spirit. Speaking in unknown tongues is not a sign that a believer has achieved the highest level in his Christian faith. It is, instead, the sign of a beginning—the beginning of God the Holy Spirit empowering the believer to do His work.

The baptism in the Holy Spirit, with the initial physical evidence of speaking in other tongues, is the promise of the Father to every Christian, regardless of age. Allow the children in your church to discover not only the divine Baptizer, but also the infilling of the Holy Spirit. Begin now by teaching this truth to the children and allow them to discover for themselves the power of the Holy Spirit!

CHAPTER 3

DO CHILDREN NEED THE BAPTISM AND CAN THEY RECEIVE IT?

A young girl attended our Christian camp for children. She was ten years old, and she did not come from a Christian family. In fact, she had only begun attending our church recently. She had never before heard the gospel message; and during the first service at camp, she accepted Jesus as her Savior.

The following day, the speaker taught about receiving the baptism in the Holy Spirit. After the message, the young girl went to the altar to pray. She continued to pray longer than most of the other children, and soon she began to praise the Lord in another language. She had been filled with the Holy Spirit with the evidence of speaking in tongues!

After the service, I asked her to tell me, in her own words, what God had done for her. She explained, "I don't know what this means; but as I was praying and asking God to fill me with His Holy Spirit, I opened my eyes and looked up. I saw a white bird fly down from the sky and land on my head. Then it disappeared. When I opened my mouth to praise Jesus, new words came out, just like the speaker said would happen!"

As I listened to her tell the story, I realized this girl could not have invented the vision of the bird coming from heaven. She had never heard the story of Jesus' baptism (See Matthew 3:13-17), nor did the speaker that night ever mention that the dove (a white bird) is one symbol the Bible uses to represent the Holy Spirit. Her experience was real. God had poured out His power in a beautiful way to this child, and He sent her a vision to explain to her what He had done.

Is the Baptism in the Holy Spirit for Children?

When God spoke through the prophet Joel about the coming outpouring of His Holy Spirit, He specifically included children.

I will pour out my Spirit on all people. Your sons and daughters will prophesy, your old men will dream dreams, your young men will see visions. Even on my servants, both men and women, I will pour out my Spirit in those days (Joel 2:28-29).

The original word in Hebrew *kol basar* literally means "all flesh." God promises that this outpouring of the Holy Spirit is for everyone: sons, daughters, old men, young men, and women. Everyone.

On the day of Pentecost, the apostle Peter stood before the confused crowd and explained the events of that day—the outpouring of the Holy Spirit and the sign of speaking in other tongues. In Acts 2:16-21, he connected Joel's prophecy to what had happened. Then he continued:

And you will receive the gift of the Holy Spirit. The promise is for you and your children and for all who are far off—for all whom the Lord our God will call (Acts 2:38-39).

Peter's words served as a reminder that the promise of the baptism in the Holy Spirit is available and would continue to be available to the listeners, their children and to the Gentiles.

Clearly, God never intended for the gift of the Holy Spirit to be available only to those over a certain age. There is no age limit given in Scripture for receiving it. Any child who has received Christ as Savior can receive the baptism in the Holy Spirit.

Do Children Need the Baptism in the Holy Spirit?

Children need the baptism in the Holy Spirit for the same reasons that adults do. They need the Holy Spirit's help to conquer sin; children are not immune to temptation. They also need His help to develop the fruit of the Spirit in their lives. They need His comfort and His teaching. And, they need power to witness.

Children filled with the Holy Spirit make very powerful and effective evangelists. They can go places that adults often can't, such as into public schools and among the children of their neighborhoods. They can speak to people who wouldn't listen to adults, and they can speak without fear or social stigma. For example, a Muslim man may hear the gospel while listening indulgently to a child speak, but that same man would not stop to listen to a pastor or missionary share the Christian message. Children need the Holy Spirit's power to take advantage of the unique opportunities they have to be witnesses.

Of course, each child develops at a different rate. Younger children may not be ready to receive or understand the Holy Spirit. However, we can still prepare their hearts to desire and receive at a later date. A farmer who waits until harvest time to plant His seeds will never see any crops. In the same way, teaching about the Holy Spirit plants seeds into children's hearts which will someday grow into a harvest.

God knows when a child is ready to receive. He will not give them something they are not ready to use. As teachers, we have a responsibility to give God every opportunity to work in a child's life. If we assume a child is too young to receive or understand the Pentecostal experience, we may rob God of the chance to do something powerful for that child.

Can Children Receive the Baptism in the Holy Spirit?

Jake was eight years old when he went to a camp for ministers' children. Jake's parents were missionaries, and Jake had accepted Jesus as His Savior when he was very young. During one special service at this camp, Jake heard about the baptism in the Holy Spirit. It wasn't the first time he'd heard about it, but this time, the message spoke to his young heart; and he asked the Lord to fill Him with His power.

Jake's teacher prayed with him, and by the time his parents came to pick him up, he was praying with other tongues. His parents prayed with him too, and soon everyone was crying tears of joy. When his parents asked him to tell them what had happened, Jake explained, "I just wanted more of God's power in my life; and when I asked, He gave it to me."

Jake's parents were turning out the lights late the next night after their children had gone to bed. Jake walked into their room weeping. Fearing that he was sick, his mother asked him what was wrong.

"I was praying in my bed," he said. "I heard God tell me that he wants me to be a missionary. He wants me to go and tell children about Jesus." Jake named a specific country—one that was closed to missionaries.

Jake's parents were overjoyed. As they sat down to pray with him, they reminded Jake that the country he was called to was a difficult place to be a missionary. Jake would need to continue praying, since missionaries aren't even allowed into that country.

A few nights later, the same thing happened again. Jake's parents were turning out the lights, and Jake came out of his bedroom with tears in his eyes. He explained, "I was praying for the children in my country, when God called me again to be a missionary there. This time, he told me to keep praying, because the country would be open for missionaries by the time I am eighteen years old."

Several years later Jake was twelve years old. He still prayed for that nation, and he still made plans to become a missionary to children; and the power of the Holy Spirit was evident in his life. He asked his friends if they knew about Jesus, and if they didn't, he told them. He shared God's love with others.

I know children need the baptism in the Holy Spirit as much as adults do. I have worked in children's ministries for more than twenty years and have seen children in many cultures overcome pressures and temptations. I have seen children win their friends, their families, and other adults to the Lord, because of the power of the Holy Spirit in their lives.

I have seen children baptized in the Holy Spirit. I saw that young girl at camp filled with power, and I listened to her tell me about the vision God gave her. Other children have been baptized at camps, during children's church services, during adult services and even in their homes.

I know that children, baptized in the Holy Spirit and nurtured in their faith, will flourish. I watch it happen every day; Jake, who was called to missions at the age of eight, is my son.

In an article addressing our Pentecostal heritage, James K. Bridges, General Treasurer of the U.S. Assemblies of God writes:

The baptism in the Holy Spirit is a major part of our Pentecostal heritage. It was the foundation on which the Assemblies of God was founded. Yet, I fear that this next generation is losing out because the Holy Spirit is taking a back seat in many children's ministries. If this next generation is to be Pentecostal, then we, as leaders, need to teach them and make sure that this heritage is passed on.

I'm challenging all of you, as leaders in children's ministry, to make the Holy Spirit a part of your teaching and a part of your services. Allow the Holy Spirit to move. Allow time for children to be filled. Encourage them to pray in tongues and to be used in the gifts of the Holy Spirit. We MUST be committed to passing on to the next generation the heritage of the Holy Spirit. It is our responsibility.[2]

---

[2] Bridges, Rev. James K. "The Baptism in the Holy Spirit," *Fanning the Flame.* The General Council of the Assemblies of God, Children's Ministries Agency, 20, (Spring 2006): 6.

CHAPTER 4

HOW DO I TEACH ABOUT THE HOLY SPIRIT?

Judy was a Sunday school teacher in a local church. She wasn't a pastor or a Bible school teacher, but she had decided that every one of her eleven and twelve-year-old students would be filled with the Holy Spirit by the time they left her class. Year after year, class after class, boys were being filled with the Holy Spirit. Some of them were filled in her classroom. Others were filled in children's church or in the adult sanctuary on a Sunday night.

How was Judy able to teach about the Holy Spirit so effectively? She prepared herself and her students, and she provided time for the Holy Spirit to work.

Prepare Yourself: Model the Holy Spirit

You cannot lead someone where you have never been yourself. Neither can you effectively lead your students into the baptism in the Holy Spirit until you receive it yourself.

If you have not received the baptism in the Holy Spirit with the evidence of speaking in tongues, now is the time to seek it. We have already shown that God desires to give this gift to every believer; this includes you!

If you then, though you are evil, know how to give good gifts to your children, how much more will your Father in heaven give the Holy Spirit to those who ask Him (Luke 11:13).

Children learn by imitation. If you model a Spirit-filled life in front of your students, they will learn from your example. In fact, students learn better by watching your example than they do by listening to your words. Exhibit the fruit of love, joy, patience, gentleness, etc., in your classroom. Allow the children to hear you and other adults praying and worshipping in your own language and in other tongues. Let them see your boldness and excitement for God in everything you do. You are an "advertisement" for the joy of a Spirit-filled life.

Rev. Charles Crabtree, former Assistant General Superintendent of the U.S. Assemblies of God, writes about his childhood:

At the earliest age, I would listen to our house guests around the table and then watch them around the house, not realizing I was making a judgment to see if they behaved as well as they spoke. You see, what they did would either enforce what they had said, or cancel everything they had spoken.[3]

Rev. Crabtree explains that children's leaders must live the definition of a Spirit-filled Christian life; otherwise, children will get a warped and inaccurate idea of Pentecost. The reason that Jesus

---

[3]Crabtree, Rev. Charles. "The Holy Spirit in Me," *Fanning the Flame.* The General Council of the Assemblies of God, Children's Ministries Agency, 20, (Spring 2006): 12-13.

made such an impact on the world is that He kept God's truth pure in His heart, and it showed to everyone around Him. He modeled truth.

Prepare the Children: Welcome the Holy Spirit

In the previous chapter, we mentioned that a farmer who waits to plant his seeds until harvest time will never see any crops. If he wants to reap a harvest, he must plant the seeds. In order to plant the seeds, he must prepare the ground. You can prepare children's hearts and plant seeds that allow the Holy Spirit to give the harvest in His time.

Welcome the Holy Spirit into every service. Let Him be a regular guest in your class and a regular part of your teaching, whether or not your lesson for that day focuses on Him. In many services, you will find "teachable moments"[4] that can be used to prepare children's hearts for the Holy Spirit. For example, during a worship service, point out the Holy Spirit's presence. While telling a Bible story, mention Him by name and show how He played a role in the story. After teaching a memory verse, remind the children that the Holy Spirit will help them remember what they have learned. When you look for ways to welcome the Holy Spirit, you will find opportunities to teach about Him.

If the Holy Spirit is continually present in your classroom, He will not be a stranger to your students. They will begin to see Him working in your life and theirs. The small 'tastes' of the Holy Spirit that you allow in class will make children hunger for more.

Prepare the Children: Teach About the Holy Spirit

In addition to recognizing His presence in every service, set aside specific times to teach about the Holy Spirit and about the baptism in the Holy Spirit. You can focus on Him during Sunday school or

---

[4] Teachable Moment: A moment that is perfect to teach a spiritual truth, but that you hadn't planned or created.

children's church once a quarter. You can set aside a special event, such as a camp or children's crusade, to focus on Him.

Allow people who have already received the baptism in the Holy Spirit to tell your students about the experience. A testimony from an adult or even from another child can serve both to teach your students about the Holy Spirit and to create a desire for the gift in their own lives.

It is important that your students are taught who the Holy Spirit is, what He does in the life of the believer, what it means to be baptized, etc. When children are exposed to the Holy Spirit and receive answers to their questions, they will begin to want to be filled with His power.

Provide Time for the Holy Spirit to Work

Before class even begins, you can allow the Holy Spirit to work. Pray for your service and as you prepare, ask the Holy Spirit to guide you. Ask Him to come and to fill your students with His power.

Then, during your service, allow time for Him to work. Allow the gifts of the Holy Spirit during your worship service. During prayer times, encourage children to worship God in the Spirit. You can lead by example; pray aloud in tongues so that the children can hear you. Encourage children who have been filled to pray for others using the new prayer languages God has given them.

Allowing the Holy Spirit to work in your service may mean that you change your lesson at the last moment. If the Spirit prompts you to make a change in your lesson plans, trust His voice to lead you. He knows much better than you what is happening in the lives of your students. Often when the Spirit interrupts you, it means that He has something much more important to do.

Provide Time for Children to Respond

Children will respond to the opportunities you give them. If you invite children to come to the altar to pray for salvation, they will. But if that is the only thing you ever invite them to pray for, they will not know to ask for anything more.

Encourage children to pray to receive the baptism in the Holy Spirit. Pray with them and allow children who have already received to pray for others. Encourage an attitude of worship, even among children who choose not to seek the baptism in the Holy Spirit, so that those who wish to pray are not distracted.

Allow enough time for children to linger and to wait on the Spirit. Even the disciples in the upper room were baptized in the Holy Spirit after several days of prayer. If you leave only a few minutes at the closing of your service, the children will not have time to seek and to listen to the voice of the Spirit. Do not try to rush the experience. However, do not try to push children to pray longer than they are able to focus their attention in prayer either. Just allow children as much time as they need to pray in an atmosphere of worship and praise.

You Can Introduce Children to the Holy Spirit

When you welcome the Holy Spirit into your services, when you show children how the Spirit has changed your life, and when you teach about Him, you give your students the opportunity to receive His life-changing gift. Rev. David Boyd, Director of the National Children's Ministries Agency of the U.S. Assemblies of God writes:

> Let me encourage you, as children's leaders, to plant the seeds of hunger for the baptism in the Holy Spirit in the hearts of your children. I know that in every service or class that you teach, children hear the message of salvation and have the opportunity to respond. But do they hear about the great gift of the baptism in the Holy

Spirit that God has for each of them? Do they hear that this gift will give them the boldness to stand up for Jesus? Do they hear about speaking in tongues, which will help them as they pray?

It's easy to bypass this special gift from God with the day-to-day preparations of lessons for your children. But let me encourage you, I have found that when you regularly give the children a taste of the Holy Spirit when you teach, they will build up a desire to be filled. That desire will become something they fervently pray about. Those fervent prayers will be answered by God as He baptizes your children in the Holy Spirit.[5]

---

[5] Boyd, Rev. David. "The Holy Spirit and Children", *Fanning the Flame*. The General Council of the Assemblies of God, Children's Ministries Agency, 20 (Spring 2006): 1-2.

CHAPTER 5

WHAT QUESTIONS DO CHILDREN ASK ABOUT THE BAPTISM?

Understanding the Holy Spirit is a difficult task. Even adults, whatever their level of education, struggle to understand. To a child, the Holy Spirit can seem both confusing and unknowable. As they try to understand Him, they will ask questions.

Welcome children's questions! It is a sign that the children are trying to learn. Children are observant and curious. To a child who has never seen the gifts of the Spirit, they may seem strange or frightening. When he asks a question, it is because there is something he does not fully understand. In this chapter, we will look more closely at questions children commonly ask about the baptism in the Holy Spirit, and how you can answer them.

What If a Child Asks a Question That I Do Not Know the Answer To?

Always answer children's questions honestly. If you do not know the answer, tell them. Say, "I don't know, but let's find out together."

Then, talk to a pastor, a teacher, or search God's Word yourself to bring an answer to the child.

Because of the limits of our human minds, we will never be able to fully understand some aspects of God. However, God is the one who gives knowledge. Proverbs 2:6 tells us, "For the Lord gives wisdom, and from his mouth come knowledge and understanding." And James 1:5 reminds us, "If any of you lacks wisdom, he should ask God who gives generously to all without finding fault, and it will be given to him."

Questions Children Ask

1. Why is it important to be filled with the Spirit?

The Holy Spirit gives you strength to resist the temptation to sin. You can call upon Him to help you do difficult things. Perhaps you have trouble with a bad temper, stubbornness, selfishness, or other problems. When you are tempted to do wrong, you can ask the Holy Spirit to help you, and He will give you strength to do it right.

The Holy Spirit will also make the Bible clear to you as you read. John 16:13 says, "When He, the Spirit of truth, is come, He will guide you into all truth." He will give you wisdom to make the right choices, and He will comfort you when you are sad.

When you are baptized, or filled with the Holy Spirit, He gives you power to witness to others. Acts 1:8 tells us, "You will receive power when the Holy Spirit comes on you; and you will be my witnesses." Perhaps you have been afraid to let your friends at school or in your neighborhood know you are a Christian. The Holy Spirit will give you the courage to tell others about Jesus.

2. Will I need to speak in another language when I'm filled?

Yes. While speaking in another language is not the main goal, it is the important proof that you have been baptized in the Spirit. See Acts 2:4; 10:44-46; and 19:6,7, to learn about others who also spoke in another language when filled with the Holy Spirit.

People like to say what they want with their voices. As you ask the Lord to take complete control of your life, you are saying, "Lord, take my voice and use it to speak as you wish." Speaking in a language that you do not know is proof that the Holy Spirit has come to live in your life and is speaking through you.

3. What language will I speak when I'm filled?

It will be a language you do not know. Perhaps you will be praising the Lord in a language someone else will understand. This was true when the disciples in Jerusalem were filled with the Holy Spirit. Or it may be a language understood only by God. Either way, your heart will be praising Him as you speak.

4. How do I ask the Lord to fill me?

First, remember that you are asking God to take control of your life. If you asked another person to live with you and share your room, you might have to rearrange things to make space for that new friend. So as you invite the Holy Spirit to come into your life more fully, look over your life. Do you have sin in your life that you need to get rid of? Should some other things be moved aside to make room for Him? He must be more important than everything else.

Begin to pray. Ask God to give you power to tell others about His love and His salvation. Praise the Lord for His love

35

in your life, for your salvation and for taking care of you each day. Tell Him how much you love Him. As you thank Jesus, ask the Holy Spirit to help you express your thankfulness more completely. Believe His promise to give you the power of the Holy Spirit when you ask for it.

When you think of all Jesus has done for you, you will realize you don't have adequate words in your language to praise Him as you would like. Ask the Holy Spirit to praise Jesus through your lips. As He does, using another language, you will be able to really express how you feel in your heart, and you will be filled with joy. When you feel the Holy Spirit begin to move in your heart then begin to speak out loud the words He puts in your mind. Don't be afraid to speak out loud in your new language because this is the proof that you have received the baptism in the Holy Spirit

Praying to the Lord in another language when you are first filled with the Holy Spirit is only the beginning of a lifetime of fellowship with the Lord. While you grow physically, be sure you also grow spiritually. You need the Holy Spirit to make you a strong, happy, Christian who pleases the Lord.

CHAPTER 6

HOW DO I HELP CHILDREN PRAY FOR THE BAPTISM?

As a children's pastor and missionary, I have seen many altar services where children were invited to be baptized in the Holy Spirit. I have seen children who were forced to come to the altar by their well-meaning teachers. I have seen children told that they must fall down on the ground to receive the Spirit. I have seen children told to repeat a "nonsense" phrase over and over again until they spoke in tongues, and I have seen children remain in their seats and not come to the altar because what was happening at the altar seemed too scary or strange. All of these unfortunate situations happened when the leaders and teachers did not give the children a clear understanding of the Holy Spirit or what they were coming to the altar to seek.

I have also seen children come to the altars by their own choice to pray. I have seen them seek the Lord and sincerely desire to be filled with the Holy Spirit's power. I have seen them pray for each other. I have seen them linger at the altars so long that when their parents came to pick them up, they were still praying. Children were baptized in the Holy Spirit, families prayed together and God worked in everyone's life.

Your preparation, your attitude and your words can make the difference between a disappointing experience and a life-changing encounter with the Holy Spirit for your students.

What Do I Need to Do to Prepare for the Altar Time?

If you want your students to pray and receive the baptism in the Holy Spirit, you must prepare well before the altar call. In fact, you must prepare before your service or class even begins. If you have not been baptized in the Holy Spirit yourself, begin to seek His power in your own life. Ask your pastor or an elder in your church to pray with you and begin to believe God for His gift.

Pray for a move of the Spirit as you prepare your lesson. Ask God to work, pray for your students and pray for God's anointing as you teach. Enter your classroom with an expectation that God will work in your students' lives that very day.

As you prepare your lesson, remember that when children come to the altar, they must clearly understand who the Holy Spirit is, why they need to be baptized in the Holy Spirit, and what they are asking God for. When the moment comes to invite children to the altar, your students will be ready to meet with God; and you will be ready to help them.

Finally, remember that only the Holy Spirit can baptize a child. You are just the vessel that God uses to teach them. Pray, prepare, and let God do the rest.

What Do I Say at Altar Time?

An altar call should be gentle, loving and positive. Many times an altar call is referred to as the "invitation." If you think of it as an invitation, you will stay away from improper attitudes, actions or words. Jesus said, "Let the children come to me...." (Matthew 19:14). He did not say, "Drag, coerce, push, force, or threaten them to come to me." An altar call should be a confident invitation for children to come and receive this gift from God. I am convinced that God desires to do more in the lives of children than we can even imagine, but we must let them respond to His voice, and not to our own.

An altar call should be clear. As we stated previously, the children must understand that they are coming to receive a gift of power from the Holy Spirit. They should understand that they can receive this gift if they have already accepted Jesus. If you have not already done so, this is a good time to have a separate prayer for children who would like to receive Jesus as their Savior.

Children should understand what they are supposed to do when they come to the altar. Explain that they only have to ask God for His gift of the Holy Spirit. Once they have asked for it, they can continue to believe that God will keep His promise. If you choose, you may read the following passage to the children:

Ask and it will be given to you; seek and you will find; knock and the door will be opened to you. For everyone who asks receives; he who seeks finds; and to him who knocks, the door will be opened. Which of you fathers, if your son asks for fish, will give him a snake instead? Or if he asks for an egg, will give him a scorpion? If you, then, though you are evil, know how to give good gifts to your children, how much more will your Father in heaven give the Holy Spirit to those who ask Him (Luke 11:11-13 NIV).

Once they have asked God for His baptism in the Spirit, encourage the children to praise and glorify God out loud. Explain to the children that God will not force you to speak in another tongue. He will not open your mouth for you; you must begin to use your voice yourself. Only then can His power overflow with new words from your mouth. When the Holy Spirit gives you the words to say, speak them out in faith.

Invite the children to come to the altar to pray. If you do not have an actual altar in your classroom, invite the children to come to the front of the class. It is important to have an area of the classroom designated for prayer so that the children must leave their seats. By moving from their seats, the children physically demonstrate the spiritual change that they are seeking.

As you invite the children, encourage them to make the choice to come to the altar on their own. They should not wait to see if their friends are going to go forward before they decide to go, and they do not need to wait for an adult to pray with them. They should respond to God's voice and begin to pray as soon as they arrive at the altar. They can stand, kneel, sit or bow in prayer; physical posture does not matter as much as the attitude of their hearts.

Remind the children that they may need to be patient and wait on the Lord. It is not likely that God will fill them with the Holy Spirit as soon as they begin to pray. Even the disciples, on the day of Pentecost, had been in prayer for many days. And while it may not take days of prayer for God to fill them, they may have to keep praying and asking. If they give up after a few minutes and return to their seats, they may miss something life-changing!

What Should Children Do at the Altar?

If you have made your altar call very clear, the children will understand what they are supposed to do before they come forward to pray. But many children will need to be encouraged while they are praying. Remind children to do the following:

Ask: They need to ask the Lord to fill them with His Holy Spirit, aloud, in their own language. They need to continue to pray and wait for the Lord to work. While they are waiting, they can praise the Lord in their own words for all He has done for them.

Believe: God has promised to give this gift to those who ask. But we must ask in faith, believing that God will keep His promise. Jesus said, "Therefore I tell you, whatever you ask for in prayer, believe that you have received it, and it will be yours" (Mark 11:24). We must believe that the words we hear in our hearts and minds are put there by the Holy Spirit.

Receive: When we hear the words from the Holy Spirit in our hearts and we are filled with His power, we should not be afraid to speak them out. Sometimes, a new prayer language begins with just a word or two. Whatever words the Holy Spirit puts in your heart, speak them out in faith. This is the first evidence that you have truly been baptized in the Holy Spirit.

Finally, remind the children to be respectful of this holy moment. Whether or not they choose to come to the altar to pray, this is not a time to talk with their friends, to play games or to distract their neighbors.

What Should Children's Workers Do at the Altar?

The altar service is the most critical time for every teacher, assistant teacher and helper in the classroom to be involved and to minister to children. The altar service represents the reason we minister to children—to allow God to work in their lives.

Every worker in your class should be prepared ahead of time for this service. Ask them to join with you in prayer the week prior to your lesson. They can pray for you as you prepare, pray for the children who will come, and pray for a sovereign move of the Holy Spirit. Jesus taught that there is power when we pray together in agreement.

Again, I tell you that if two of you on earth agree about anything you ask for, it will be done for you by my Father in heaven. For where two or three come together in my name, there am I with them (Matthew 18:19-20 NIV).

If your children's workers have not been filled with the Holy Spirit, they should begin to seek the Baptism themselves. If you choose, you can gather your workers together for prayer specifically for the Holy Spirit at a separate time and location from your children's service. You may even wish to invite the pastor to come and pray with you.

When the time comes to invite children to the altar, children's workers should come to the altar as well. They can pray with children, one at a time, and pray aloud in their own prayer language. As children hear others praying out loud in tongues, they will become more comfortable speaking out in prayer themselves.

We have emphasized in previous chapters that speaking with other tongues is the initial physical evidence of the baptism in the Holy Spirit. Other evidences may occur such as the sound of a rushing mighty wind, prophesies, visions, crying, laughing, and tears. Many boys and girls have wept and pled, only to receive the Baptism after they have calmed down. But altar workers will know that a child has been filled to overflowing with God's Holy Spirit as that child begins to speak in another tongue as the Spirit enables him to do so.

Altar workers should also be available to answer children's questions and encourage them. They should not tell children what to say, or tell children that they have been filled. Instead, when they hear a child praying in tongues, they can ask the child if they are speaking in tongues. If the answer is "yes," ask the child to explain what the Holy Spirit has done in his life. When the child explains in his own words, the experience becomes more real to him; and the Holy Spirit receives the credit.

If appropriate, altar workers may use a gentle touch to let the children know someone is praying for them. A hand on their shoulder, back, or head is all that is necessary. It is not acceptable to push a child down, to hold them down, or to use any type of force to imitate an experience with the Holy Spirit. The Holy Spirit is always gentle and never forces Himself on anyone. We should do the same.

Finally, altar workers should be watchful of distractions in the room. Remind children who are not praying at the altars to be respectful. Gently reseat or remove children who are distracting others rather than praying.

When and How Should I Close the Service?

It is not always perfectly clear when the time is right to close the altar service and dismiss the children. In nearly every altar service I've been in, some children finish praying quickly and return to their seats while others continue to seek the Lord wholeheartedly. Often, the decision to close the service comes either when parents begin to arrive to pick up their children or when there are many children waiting in their seats, and they are growing restless and distracting others.

Closing your altar service with a positive word is important. When you sense that the time is right to speak a final word, address those still praying by gently telling them that the altar is open as long as they want to remain in prayer.

Remind those children who have left the altar without being baptized in the Holy Spirit that God heard their prayers and that His presence has visited them, whether or not they spoke in other tongues. He will fill them when they are ready to receive His gift, and sometimes it happens at surprising moments. A girl in one camp prayed every night. It wasn't until she was at home with her mom and dad that God allowed her to pray in tongues. As a result, Mom and

Dad were both baptized in the Spirit as the girl laid hands on them. Encourage these children to walk in faith and continue asking the Lord for the Holy Spirit's power.

Explain to the children who were filled with the Holy Spirit and spoke in tongues that they can start or stop praying in tongues at any time. Their prayer language is a gift that was given to them by the Holy Spirit and is under their control. It is a language to be used in prayer every day.

Invite children who were filled with the Holy Spirit to give testimonies. Let them explain in their own words what happened to them. Their story will encourage other children that this was a real experience, and they can have it too.

An altar service is a life-changing event. It is a sacred moment when the presence of God visits your classroom and works in your children's lives. I pray that you will always be compelled to bring your children to the altars and that you will be honored to witness these moments.

CHAPTER 7

HOW DO I HELP CHILDREN GROW IN THE SPIRIT?

A young man was working as an apprentice in his father's carpenter shop. On his fifteenth birthday, his father presented him a gift—a beautiful set of carpenter's tools. The boy decided, "I am ready to open my own workshop. Thanks to my father's gift, I have everything I need. I can build furniture just like my father." He left his father's workshop to begin on his own.

But very soon, it became evident that the boy was not ready to build furniture. He could not cut the boards straight. When he tried to sand the boards smooth, he lost patience and gave up. His bookcases and desks were not sturdy and strong.

Frustrated, the boy went back to his father. "Father, why is this not working? You gave me these beautiful tools. So why can I not do my job successfully?"

"Son," the father wisely replied, "I gave you the tools you needed to be successful. But you never took the time to learn how to use them."

When a believer is baptized in the Holy Spirit, he is being equipped to do a job. The power that the Holy Spirit brings into our lives is the tool to help us to reach out to others and to tell them about God's plan of salvation. Just like the carpenter's son, before we can be truly successful at this job, we need to learn how to use the tool.

The experience your students have at the altar is just the beginning; it is your responsibility to help them grow and mature in the Spirit. Children can practice using the gift of the Holy Spirit in your services in three simple ways.

Spread the Joy

Celebrate when a child is baptized in the Holy Spirit. Tell others and encourage the child to tell others as well. Allowing children to stand up and share their testimony with other children and adults will build their faith. It will reinforce to the child that God truly has worked in their life. Their testimony will encourage others to seek the same gift.

Pray Daily

Look for opportunities to let the children pray in their new prayer languages during your children's services. An ideal time is during the worship and praise service, but it isn't the only occasion. Ask the Lord to direct you and allow the children time to develop their relationship with the Holy Spirit.

Encourage children who receive the Holy Spirit to take time daily to let the Holy Spirit pray through them in tongues every day. This "edifies" or builds up each believer (1 Corinthians 14:4). Children who have experienced the power of the Holy Spirit at the altars need to be reminded that the same power goes with them when they go to church, when they go to school, or when they go home.

Use the Gift

Give children a chance to begin using the power of the Holy Spirit to do real ministry. This allows them to grow. Allow them to help lead, and even plan, the worship service. Train a team of children to do skits or puppet ministry, and let them lead an outreach in your neighborhood. Give older children a chance to help minister in the classes of younger children.

Let God show you how you can give children opportunities to be bold witnesses and to exercise their "spiritual muscles."

God has given every person different gifts and abilities to be used in ministry to others (See 1 Corinthians 12:7-11; Ephesians 4:11,12; and Romans 12:6-8). When Spirit-filled children are allowed to practice using the power God has given them, the Holy Spirit can show the children their unique gifts within the body of Christ.

When you create an atmosphere where children can experience the power of Pentecost, you help them grow into powerful Spirit-filled believers. These believers will fulfill the mission of God—to take His message of salvation to the ends of the earth!

PART 2:

LESSON PLAN FOR TEACHING CHILDREN ABOUT THE BAPTISM IN THE HOLY SPIRIT

THE BAPTISM IN THE HOLY SPIRIT

*The baptism in the Holy Spirit is a gift of power that God
gives us to be witnesses for Him.*

Lesson Outline

1. **Opening Game/Activity: "Power Pull"**
   Have teams pull a big pile of bricks using a rope. Help one team
   pull the bricks to demonstrate that God gives us power to do the
   job He wants us to do.

2. **Character/ Puppet Skit: "The Gift of the Holy Spirit"**
   Pull objects that represent what the Holy Spirit does for us out of
   a box while the comic character misunderstands the meaning of
   each object.

3. **Verse Activity: "Power Passage, Acts 1:8"**
   Ask children to recite the verse after hearing it just twice, then
   give them help by acting out the verse.

4. **Bible Story: "Before and After"**
   Tell the story of Simon Peter as two separate characters: Simon
   and Peter. Show the difference in his life before and after the
   Baptism in the Holy Spirit.

5. **Object Lesson 1: "Clean or Dirty"**
   Use clean and dirty glasses to show that the Holy Spirit will only
   fill a clean heart.

6. **Object Lesson 2: "On the Shelf"**
   Fill a glass and set it aside without drinking it to explain that the
   Holy Spirit will not fill someone who will not use His gift.

7. **Object Lesson 3: "Is It Full?"**
   Demonstrate that when a glass overflows, it is completely filled. Explain that when we are completely filled with the Holy Spirit, we will overflow.

8. **Altar: "The Baptism in the Holy Spirit"**
   Encourage children to seek the Baptism in the Holy Spirit.

1. OPENING GAME/ACTIVITY: "POWER PULL"

Have teams pull a big pile of bricks using a rope. Help one team pull the bricks to demonstrate that God gives us power to do the job He wants us to do.

Participants:

- Teacher

- Two teams of three children each

Props:

- A pile of cement blocks (5-10)

- A rope

- Something to mark lines on the floor – a "start" and a "finish" line

Preparation:

- Mark two lines on the floor in the front of the classroom approximately three meters (ten feet) apart. Tie the rope securely to the cement blocks—only tie as many as you can pull. Place the blocks on the "start" line. Lay the rope across the floor to the "finish" line.

What to Do:

Choose two teams of three children each. Make sure that one team has smaller children and won't be as strong as the other team. Explain that each team must stand behind the finish line and only use the rope to pull the blocks from the start line to the finish line. The team that does it the fastest will win. Tell the other children in the class to cheer for the team that they think will win.

Allow the team of bigger children to go first. Give them a starting signal, and time them using a watch or by counting the seconds out loud. When the blocks cross the finish line, announce their time to the class.

Return the blocks to the start line and have the second team of smaller children take their place. Give them a starting signal. After a couple of seconds have passed, step forward quickly and grab the rope near the blocks. Help the children pull the blocks across the finish line as quickly as possible. Announce the second team's time and declare them the winners.

The first team, and perhaps many of the other children in the class, will probably complain that helping the second team was unfair. Explain that this game is an example of what we are going to learn about in our lesson today.

Tell the children that God has given us a job to do. Just like the first team, we can try to do the job in our own strength, and we may even succeed. But God wants to help us. He wants to give us more power to do the job better than we could on our own. In the same way, the teacher helped the second team to be better and more powerful so that they were able to do more than they could in their own strength.

Tips:

- Use this game as a reward for children who are behaving well in class. Tell everyone that you only choose volunteers who pay attention and obey the rules of the class.

- Keep the explanation short at the end of the game. This is just an introduction to the main idea of the lesson. Later, you will explain the job that God has given to us and how we receive His power to do it. By not explaining everything now, you will keep the children interested in what comes next in the lesson.

- Tell the children that if there is time at the end of the lesson, you will allow more teams to play, seeing which team can pull the blocks the fastest. This will allow you to keep the children's minds on the lesson and to fill extra time constructively at the end of the lesson.

- Make sure the blocks are securely tied to the rope. If you can find blocks with holes all the way through, attach them securely by passing the rope through the holes.

2. CHARACTER/PUPPET SKIT: "THE GIFT OF THE HOLY SPIRIT"

Pull objects that represent what the Holy Spirit does for us out of a box while the comic character misunderstands the meaning of each object.

Participants:

- Teacher

- Comedy character (This can be either someone in a costume or a puppet, depending on what you have available.)

Props:

- A map

- A piece of fruit

- A hammer

- A doll

- A school textbook

- A battery (as big as possible)

- A box or bag big enough to hold all the objects listed above

- A puppet, or a funny costume for a live comedy character. (The rest of this lesson will refer to a puppet, but you can replace the puppet with a helper dressed in a funny costume if you prefer.)

Preparation:

- Copy the list below onto a small piece of paper:

Map	=	Guide	John 16:13
Fruit	=	Fruit of the Spirit	Galatians 5:22
Hammer	=	Tools	Corinthians 12:7-11
Doll	=	Comfort	John 14:16
School Book	=	Training	John 14:26
Battery	=	Power	Acts 1:8

- Tape the list to the inside of the box where you can easily read it. If you would like, you can decorate the box to look like a gift. Tape a sign that says "HOLY SPIRIT" on the outside of the box.

- Practice the skit as many times as possible with the puppet.

What to Do:

Bring out the box, but don't show the children the side with the "Holy Spirit" sign. Ask the children if they like gifts. God has many gifts for us, but we want to learn about a very special gift today. It is one gift that is really many things. Would anyone like to see what I have in my box? *(This is the cue for the puppet to enter.)*

Puppet: *(Enter the stage shouting...)* "Me, me, show me what's in the box. I want to see."

Teacher: *(Calm the puppet down and ask...)* "What is your name?"

Puppet: "My name is Agbay." (*Use whatever name you prefer.*)

Teacher: "Well Agbay, if you'll be calm, I'll show you and all the children what is in the box. This box represents God's gift of the Holy Spirit. *(Turn the box around to show the sign.)* The Holy Spirit is actually many gifts, because He does many things for us. I have some things in this box that will show us some of the things that the Holy Spirit does for us. Would you like to see them?"

Puppet: "Yes, yes please show us. Oh please, oh please, oh please, oh pleeeeeeaaaassse show us."

Teacher: "Alright, alright Agbay. Don't get upset, I'll show you. The first gift of the Holy Spirit is…this!" *(Pull the map out of the box.)*

Puppet: "A map? I don't need a map. I know where I am. I'm…I'm uhh…I'm…ahh! I'm right here. See? I know exactly where I am. I don't need a map."

Teacher: "Agbay, the Holy Spirit doesn't give us a real map. The map represents a gift of the Holy Spirit. That gift is direction. John 16:13 says that the Holy Spirit guides and directs our lives."

Puppet: "Just like a map gives us direction."

Teacher: "Yes, just like a map. But that's not all the Holy Spirit does for us. Look at what else I have in the box." *(Put the map down, and pull the piece of fruit out of the box.)*

Puppet: "Yeah, snack time! Give me! Give me! I'm starving."

Teacher: "No Agbay, it's not a snack. This fruit reminds us that one of the Holy Spirit's gifts to us is fruit. When we talk about the fruit of the Spirit, we mean the good things that the Holy Spirit causes to grow in our hearts- things like love, joy, peace, patience and many more that are listed in Galatians 5:22 and in other verses."

Puppet: "So we can't eat the Holy Spirit fruit?"

Teacher: "No. But if you are good, I'll let you eat this after the lesson. Now let's see what other gifts the Holy Spirit has for us. *(Put down the fruit and pull the hammer out of the box.)*

Puppet: *(When Agbay sees the hammer, he screams and ducks.)*

Teacher: "Agbay! What's wrong? Why are you so frightened?"

Puppet: *(Talk in a scared, shaky voice.)* "Keep it away from me. It doesn't like me."

Teacher: "What? The hammer?" *(Hold out the hammer toward the puppet. He should scream and duck again. You can have fun with this and repeat this several times.)* "What's the matter with you? It's just a hammer. It won't attack you."

Puppet: "Yes it will. It doesn't like me. Every time I get near a h-h-hammer, it hits me. It hits me on the toe or the finger, and sometimes even on the head. How can something so dangerous be a gift of the Holy Spirit?"

Teacher: "Well it's not really that dangerous if you're careful. The reason I have it in the gift box is because it is a tool. First Corinthians 12:7-11 tells us that the Holy Spirit gives us tools that we can use to help everyone in the church."

Puppet: "Okay, Okay, I understand. Holy Spirit…tools…good gift! Now please put that scary thing away."

Teacher: "Alright (Put hammer down.), but I do have something that isn't nearly so scary." (Pull the doll out of the box.)

Puppet: "Dolly! Hey where'd you get my dolly? Please give it back. I need my dolly." *(Teacher holds out the doll, and the puppet snuggles up to it.)* "Oh dolly, I missed you so much."

Teacher: "Does that doll make you feel good? Does it bring you comfort?"

Puppet: "Oh yes, Dolly always makes me feel better."

Teacher: "Well good. I'm glad you feel better. And that's just what the Holy Spirit does for us. John 14:16 tells us that the Holy Spirit is our Comforter. He makes us feel better when we face problems or hard times. *(Teacher starts to put the doll down, but Agbay cries.)* Now Agbay, you can have your doll back after the lesson, but we have a couple more gifts to look at." *(Put down the doll, and pull the school book out of the box.)*

Puppet: "What! A school book? That's a terrible gift. Nobody likes to study."

Teacher: "That's not true, Agbay. Some people like to study. And even more importantly, everyone needs to study and learn. Do you want people to think you are ignorant?"

Puppet: "Hey! Are you calling me stupid?"

Teacher: "No, but if you never learn anything, then people will never think you are very smart. This book is a reminder that we need to learn. We need to be trained. And the Bible tells us in John 14:26 that the Holy Spirit will teach us." *(Put the school book down.)*

Puppet: "Wow, the Holy Spirit sure gives us a lot of gifts."

Teacher: "Yes and there are more gifts we could talk about today. But, I just want to mention one more. It is a very important gift, and it is the one that we are going to talk about today. That gift is represented by this." *(Pull the battery out of the box.)*

Puppet: "A battery! What does that mean? Is the Holy Spirit going to shock us? Or charge us up?"

Teacher: "Shock us – no. The Holy Spirit is a gift to help us, not to hurt us. But you were close when you said He charges us up. The last gift of the Holy Spirit is power. Just like this battery gives us power to do a job, the Holy Spirit gives us power to do a job. Acts 1:8 tells us that God will give us power from on high. Today, we are going to learn about that power and how we can receive it."

Puppet: "Power sounds good. I like power. So how exactly do I get this power?"

Teacher: "I'll be glad to tell you. In fact, I'm going to tell everyone here about the power of the Holy Spirit. You sit back quietly, eat your snack and listen to the rest of our lesson."

Puppet: "Okay, and I'll take Dolly too."

Teacher: "Okay, the gifts of the Holy Spirit that we've talked about are here." *(Teacher puts box behind puppet stage.)*

Puppet: *(Agbay exits and we hear his voice from off stage.)* "Ahh! This snack is delicious, isn't it Dolly? And look at all these cool gifts. There's the book and the map and AAAAAHHHH! No! Not the hammer. Get it away from me…get it awaaaayyy."

Tips:

- Have fun with this skit. The comedy character especially should be silly and make the children laugh. But don't let the classroom get out of control. Remember, the point of this skit is to introduce the lesson and teach the children a spiritual truth.

- Don't read the script. Practice it enough that the only note you need is the list taped to the inside of the box. It will appear more natural if you don't try to read the whole script.

3. VERSE ACTIVITY: "POWER PASSAGE, ACTS 1:8"

Ask children to recite the verse after hearing it just twice, then give them help by acting out the verse.

Participants:

- Teacher

- The whole class

Props:

- Your Bible

- A list of all the motions for the verse *(See preparation step.)*

Preparation: Copy the list below onto a piece of paper.

- **But you**... *(Point towards children.)*

- **will receive**...*(Hold cupped hands out in front of you and then draw them in towards yourself.)*

- **power**...*(Flex your muscles.)*

- **when the Holy Spirit**... *(Put your thumbs together, one on top of the other, and flap your fingers like wings as you raise your hands above your head like a bird.)*

- **comes on you**...*(Keep flapping your hands like a bird, and bring it down to land on your head.)*

- **and you**...*(Point towards children.)*

- **will be my witnesses**...*(Bunch your fingers together in front of your mouth, and then move your hand outward and open your fingers at the same time, as if words are coming out of your mouth.)*

- **Acts 1:8**... *(Hold up one finger and then hold up eight fingers.)*

Use this paper as a bookmark in your Bible to mark Acts 1:8.

What to Do:

Explain to the children that they need to learn what the Bible says about the power of the Holy Spirit. So, they are going to memorize an important Bible verse. Tell them you want to see if they can do it all by themselves. Have them listen carefully as you read the verse slowly and clearly.

Read the verse a second time, adding the actions as you say the words. Now have the children try to say the verse by themselves (*You may have to say the first two words to get them started in unison.*) As they say the verse, you can do the actions to remind them what comes next.

After they finish, encourage the children that they did a good job. Ask them if they received any help. *(Allow responses. You want them to talk about the help you gave them with your actions.)*

Explain that the Holy Spirit gives us a job to do—to be a witness to the whole world. But He also gives us help—the power to do that job. We receive that power when we are baptized in the Holy Spirit.

Ask them to say the verse again with you. This time, encourage everyone to do the actions. Repeat the verse several times and then have them try to do it on their own.

After they have memorized the verse, tell them that we have learned what God's Word says, and now we are going to learn how that applies to our lives. We are going to learn how we can be baptized in the Holy Spirit and receive the power to be witnesses for God.

Tips:

- Remember that the point of this game/activity is to teach every child the verse. The actions help reinforce the learning. Be sure that all the children are doing the actions. Be encouraging.

- For younger children, you may have to repeat the verse several times with the actions before they can do it on their own.

4. BIBLE STORY: "BEFORE AND AFTER"

Tell the story of Simon Peter as two separate characters: Simon and Peter. Show the difference in his life before and after the Baptism in the Holy Spirit.

Participants:

- Teacher

- The whole class will answer questions

Props:

- Simon/Peter face cutout *(See diagram in the preparation step.)*

- Chalkboard & chalk *(Or another means of drawing pictures for all children to see.)*

Preparation:

- Make a Simon/Peter face cutout prop using the following instructions. Use a small plate or another round object of similar size to trace two touching circles on a large piece of paper. The circles should be as big as possible so that the children can easily see the faces and words.

- Use a paper that is heavy enough that the words on one side will not show through to the other side. If you don't have thick paper, cut two of the double circles, draw the images, one side on each separate piece of paper, and glue the two pieces together back-to-back. The two sides of this paper are drawn below.

- After you have finished drawing and writing on both sides of the cutout shape, fold it in half. Make sure the faces are on the outside and the words are hidden inside.

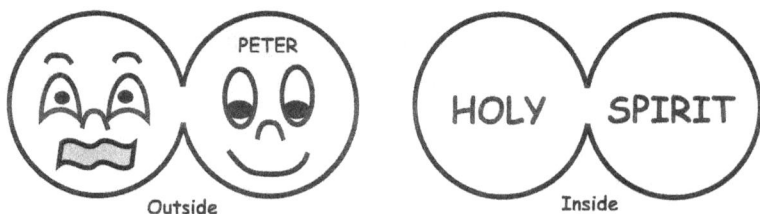

Outside   Inside

- Review the drawings included after the story. Draw 13 blank circles on the chalkboard before class begins. These are the circles you will use to draw all the pictures. Make them as large as possible, so that the whole class can see them.

- Read Acts 1-2. Review the story, and practice re-telling it using the drawings.

What to Do:

Bring out the Simon/Peter face cutout, folded closed to hide the inside. Tell the children that you are going to tell them a story about two men. The first one, named Simon, was a cowardly man. (*Show the children the "Simon" face.*) The second man, named Peter, was a bold man. (*Turn the face around to show children the "Peter" face.*)

Before beginning the story, ask the children to help you learn a little bit more about Simon and Peter by playing a game. Read a statement from the list below, and ask the children to tell you if they believe the statement describes Simon, the cowardly man, or Peter, the bold man. Each time you reveal the correct answer, show the corresponding face on the cutout.

- This man, after following Jesus for three years, denied even knowing Him. (*Simon*)

- This man, after being told by the religious leaders not to speak about Jesus, immediately began preaching about Him again. (*Peter*)

- This man preached to a crowd of three-thousand people. (*Peter*)

- This man was afraid to tell a little girl that he knew Jesus. (*Simon*)

- This man hid from Roman soldiers after Jesus had been crucified. (*Simon*)

- This man was sentenced to death for preaching about Jesus, but God sent an angel to break him out of prison. As soon as he left the prison, he began teaching about Jesus again. (*Peter)*

Tell the children that although Simon and Peter seem like completely opposite men, they are actually the same man. Simon was a disciple of Jesus. Before Jesus returned to heaven, He changed Simon's name to Peter. *(As you talk, turn the cutout back and forth from the Simon face to the Peter face.)*

How did one man change from being afraid of confessing Jesus to a little child, to preaching about Jesus, even when he knew that he might be killed for it? Something happened to change Simon Peter on the inside. Something happened that gave him the power to speak boldly about Jesus.

(Open the cutout and show the children the words "Holy Spirit" written on the inside). It was the gift of power, the Holy Spirit filling Simon Peter, which changed Him.

Bible Story:

Set aside the cutout. Tell the story of Peter and the day of Pentecost from Acts 1-2, drawing a picture in each of the 13 circles as shown in the drawing guide below. Finish the drawing at the correct point in the story, following the outline below. Fill in extra details in the story based on your reading of the scriptures.

Picture 1:

- After Jesus rose from the dead, He took His disciples to a mountaintop.

- There, He told them to go to the whole world and make more disciples.

- But first, He told them to wait and pray until they received a gift from God, a gift that would give them power.

- The disciples watched, amazed, as Jesus was lifted up into heaven.

Picture 2:

- While they were still watching the sky, an angel appeared to the disciples.

- The angel said to them, "Why are you watching the sky? Jesus has been taken into heaven, but He will return one day in the same way you saw Him leave."

- So the disciples left the mountain and returned to Jerusalem.

Picture 3:

- They remembered that Jesus had told them to wait and to pray until they received a gift from God - a gift of power.

- So they began to pray.

Picture 4:

- They prayed for one hour.

- Do you know what happened after one hour?

Picture 5:

- Nothing happened.

Picture 6:

- So they kept on praying.

Picture 7:

- They prayed for hours and hours—all day long.

- Do you know what happened after one full day?

Picture 8:

- Nothing happened.

Picture 9:

- So they kept on praying, and praying and praying.

Picture 10:

- They prayed for days.

- And do you know what happened?

Picture 11:

- This time, something happened.

- They heard a sound like the wind blowing. The sound filled the whole house.

Picture 12:

- They saw what looked like tongues of fire that came to rest on everyone's head.

Picture 13:

- Everyone there was filled with the Holy Spirit and began to speak in languages they had never learned, because the Holy Spirit gave them the power.

Conclusion:

(Pick up the Simon/Peter cutout prop.) This event, which we call the Day of Pentecost, is what changed Simon, the cowardly man *(Show the "Simon" face.)* into Peter, the bold man. *(Show the "Peter" face.)*

The Holy Spirit came and filled the disciples with power to preach the Good News boldly. On that very same day, Peter preached a powerful message and 3,000 people heard and believed the message.

In the weeks and months that followed, Peter continued to preach boldly, even after he was threatened, thrown in jail and even sentenced to death. Nothing could stop him, because he had the power of the Holy Spirit inside him. (*Open the cutout prop again to show the children the "Holy Spirit" inside.*)

Tips for Drawing Pictures:

- Practice drawing the pictures before you do it in front of the class. You should be able to draw while you talk. The pictures are drawn very simply so that you can draw while you are talking.

- Use the paper with the pictures drawn on it as a reminder if you need it, but remember that the most important thing in telling a story is to not read it. Keep eye contact with the children whenever you're not actually drawing.

- See Picture Drawing Guide on next page.

Picture Drawing Guide

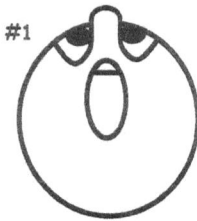

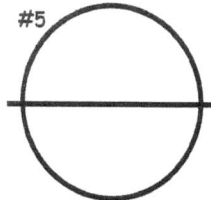

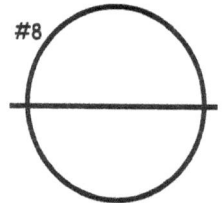

5. OBJECT LESSON 1: "CLEAN OR DIRTY"

Use clean and dirty glasses (cups) to show that the Holy Spirit will only fill a clean heart.

Participants:

- Teacher

Props:

- An opaque glass or cup

- Mud

- A towel

- A tub of dish water and a dish rag

- A pitcher of water

- A tray with 5 or 6 glasses on it

Preparation:

- Spread the mud around the inside of the opaque glass or cup. Leave a small clean edge at the top edge. Be sure that none of the mud shows from the outside. You don't want the children to know that the inside of the glass is muddy until you turn it towards them.

- Place the pitcher of water and all the glasses on the tray and cover them with the towel.

What to Do:

Tell the children that we have seen in our story what a difference the power of the Holy Spirit can make. Now we are going to learn how we can be baptized in the Holy Spirit and use His power to be witnesses.

(Bring out the tray with the glasses and the pitcher of water. Place it on a table or chair and remove the towel. Make sure that the children cannot see into the dirty glass.)

(Pick up the pitcher of water.) Tell the children that this pitcher of water represents the Holy Spirit. The Bible compares the Spirit of God to water in verses like Isaiah 44:3.

(Now pick up the dirty glass, keeping the inside hidden.) The glasses represent our lives. The Holy Spirit wants to fill us with His power, but He won't waste His power, just as you wouldn't waste water filling up this glass. *(Act as if you are going to pour water into the glass, but stop before you actually pour any into the glass.)* Why would it be a waste? Because no one would actually want to drink out of this glass. *(Turn the glass towards the children and show them the inside.)*

(Next, pour a little water into the glass and show the children the muddy water.) Explain that it would be wasteful to pour pure water into a dirty glass: Would anyone want to actually drink the water out of this glass? What would you need to do before filling the glass and drinking out of it? *(Allow children to respond that the glass needs to be washed.)*

(Bring out the wash basin and begin to wash the glass.) Explain to the children that the dirty glass represents our lives. Sin makes our hearts dirty, just like the inside of the glass. Before we can be filled with the power of the Holy Spirit, we must be cleaned out. This is salvation. When we ask Jesus to forgive us for all the bad things we have done, He cleans our heart and takes away the sin.

(Show the children the clean, inside of the glass.) Explain that the first thing that must happen if we want to be baptized in the Holy

Spirit is that we must ask Jesus to save us from our sins. After our hearts are clean, we can ask the Holy Spirit to fill us. (*At this point, pour some water into the clean glass.*)

Tell the children this is only the first thing we must do to be baptized in the Holy Spirit, and then move on to the next illustration.

Tips:

- Remember that the objects you hold in your hands are what draws and keeps the interest of the children. Don't put the objects down. Learn to talk as you wash and pour the water.

- This illustration works best if you don't show the inside of the dirty glass until the last minute. Make sure the mud is thickly coated and has dried enough to stick to the sides of the glass.

6. Object Lesson 2: "On the Shelf"

Fill a glass and set it aside without drinking it to explain that the Holy Spirit will not fill someone who will not use His gift.

Participants:

- Teacher

Props:

- The pitcher of water from the first illustration

- A piece of paper and some tape

- The glasses from the first illustration

Preparation:

- Draw a face on the paper that is big enough to cover half the glass. Tape it on one side of the glass and place this glass behind the others where it cannot be seen.

What to Do:

Tell the children that there is something else that is very important to understand if we want to be baptized in the Holy Spirit. (*Pick up the glass with the face on it*). Let's look at another glass as an example. Imagine that this glass could talk and make choices just like us. (*Turn the glass around and show the children the face.*)

Next, have a pretend conversation with the glass. The glass will tell you how much he wants to be filled with water, and you will ask him why. The glass will keep telling you how special it will make him feel and that he just wants to be filled. You try to explain that your water is supposed to be used to help others – those who are thirsty. But the glass doesn't listen to you. He just keeps insisting on being filled. Finally, you give him some water.

Turn the glass away from you and move it like it is walking away. Continue talking to the glass and ask him where he is going. The glass will tell you that he has what he wants, and now he is going to go rest on his shelf. Try to explain to him that you filled him up to be used, but he won't listen and just leaves.

Now turn to the children, and tell them that you were just having fun with this little skit. But, sadly, the glass is like many Christians. We say that we want to be baptized in the Holy Spirit and filled with His power, but we don't really want to do anything with His gift. We just want to feel good.

The Bible tells us that we are given the power of the Holy Spirit so that we can do a job. Ask the children what that job is. Encourage them to remember the verse they have learned, until they answer that we are supposed to be witnesses for God.

Explain that the Holy Spirit will not waste His power on someone who is not planning to use it. If you are not planning to be a witness for Him, then you don't need His special power. If you plan to just "sit on a shelf" and do nothing, then you don't need His gift. But, if you really want to do God's work and be a witness for Him, you need to be baptized in the Holy Spirit and receive His special power.

Review with the children the two things we need to do in order to be baptized in the Holy Spirit: 1) be saved and 2) be ready to use His power. Move on to the third illustration.

Tips:

- If you have a puppet stage that you used for the comedy character skit, you can do this illustration as another puppet skit. When you say that you need another glass at the beginning of the illustration, this will be the cue for your helper to bring up the "face" glass from behind the stage. Then, he will provide the voice of the glass. Don't worry if the children can see his hand. This will just make the skit funnier.

- This is a silly idea – talking to a glass. But if you have fun with it, the children will have fun watching you do it. Enjoy yourself and don't worry about looking foolish.

7. OBJECT LESSON 3: "IS IT FULL?"

Demonstrate that when a glass overflows, it is completely filled. Explain that when we are completely filled with the Holy Spirit, we will overflow.

Participants:

- Teacher

Props:

- Glasses from previous illustration
- Pitcher of water from previous illustration
- Tray

Preparation:

- No extra preparation is necessary for this illustration.

What to Do:

Tell the children that they have already seen and learned about what is necessary to be baptized in the Holy Spirit. Now you would like to talk about how a person knows when he has been filled with the power of the Holy Spirit.

(Pick up another glass. Make sure it is opaque, and that the children cannot see what is inside.) Remind the children that this glass represents our lives.

(Pick up the pitcher of water.) Ask the children to tell you when they think the glass is full. *(Hold the glass over the tray and begin to pour water slowly into the glass.)* Keep asking the children to raise their hands when they think it is full. *(When the glass is about half full, pour even more slowly, as if you are running out of space, and then stop pouring.)*

Ask the children to raise their hands if they think the glass is full now. Why do you think it is full? Can you be sure that the glass is full? *(Allow responses.)* Tell them that the glass is not full, that you can prove it. *(Slowly pour more water into the glass. Stop pouring again, while pretending as if the glass is full.)*

Once again, ask the children to raise their hands if they think the glass is full now. Why do you think it is full? Can you be sure that the glass is full? *Allow responses.* Tell them that they are wrong again. (*Continue pouring. Repeat this process until you have only one centimeter of space left at the top of the glass.*)

Tell the children that there is one sure sign that the glass is full. There is one way that everyone will see and know without doubt. (*Start slowly pouring the water again.*) Tell me when the glass is completely full by raising your hand. (*Keep pouring until the glass overflows.*) At this point, the children will all respond that the glass is obviously full.

Ask the same questions as before. Do you think the glass is full? Why do you think so? Can you be sure? *Allow responses.* Explain that this is the same with the Baptism in the Holy Spirit. God has given us a sign that lets everyone see and know, without a doubt, that our lives have been filled with the power of the Holy Spirit.

This sign is speaking in tongues. When our lives are completely filled with the Holy Spirit, they begin to overflow, just like the glass. What comes pouring out of us is the gift of speaking in tongues. Speaking in tongues is a special prayer language that God gives us. We don't understand what we are saying, but the Spirit of God is speaking through us. This is a sign to us and to everyone around us that we really have been filled with His power and are ready to use that power to be witnesses for Him.

Tell the children that we have learned what we need to do in order to receive the baptism in the Holy Spirit. We have also learned how we know when we have received this gift. Now we are going to pray and ask God to give us the gift of the Holy Spirit.

Tips:

- Remember the focus of the lesson. It is easy at this point to want to explain more about the Holy Spirit, and there is much more for the children to learn. However, remember that this lesson is only about the baptism in the Holy Spirit. If you try to teach them too many other points about the Holy Spirit, you may end up confusing them.

- This illustration is very visual and explains itself. Don't spend too much time talking. Move quickly into the altar/prayer time, and give the children plenty of time to respond to what the Holy Spirit is doing in their lives.

8. ALTAR:
"BAPTISM IN THE HOLY SPIRIT"

Encourage children to seek the baptism in the Holy Spirit.

Participants:

- Teacher
- All the children

Props:

- Glasses from previous illustrations
- Pitcher of water from previous illustrations

Preparation:

- No additional preparation for the altar time is necessary.

What to Do:

Remind the children that today we have been studying God's gift of the Holy Spirit, and especially, the part of this gift that we call the "Baptism in the Holy Spirit," when the Holy Spirit fills us with power so that we can be witnesses for Him.

Tell the children that they are going to have a chance to be baptized in the Holy Spirit. There are three important things to remember as they ask to be filled. They should:

Open their hearts – (Hold an empty glass upside down.) Show the children how the glass, when it is upside down, cannot be filled with water. Unless you open your heart to God, you will not be filled. (*Turn the glass the right way up and pour a little water into it.*)

Open their mouths – in other words, encourage children to pray out loud. (*Hold the glass by placing your hand over the mouth of the glass.*) Show the children that with the glass covered, it cannot get any fuller and nothing can come out. When you begin to pray, at first you will pray in words you understand. As you are filled with the Holy Spirit, you will begin to speak in another language. But the language cannot come out if you keep your mouths shut. Encourage everyone who wants to pray to do it out loud.

Wait – this is probably the most important thing for children to understand as they are praying. Too often, they pray for a short time and then give up. Encourage the children to keep praying until the Holy Spirit fills them. (*Hold up the glass and fill it just a bit more.*) Tell the children that when we ask God for His power, He begins to fill us. (*Pour a bit more water in the glass.*) Every time we ask, God hears our prayers and fills us a bit more. (*Pour some more water in the glass.*)

Some people are filled very quickly because they are ready to be filled. But, for other people, it can take time. (*Pour more water in the glass.*) We need to allow the Holy Spirit the time He needs to work in our lives. If we give Him enough time and we are ready to use His gift; we will be filled. (*Pour in enough water to overflow the glass.*) We will have the evidence of being filled, which is speaking in tongues.

Invite the children to pray. You and other leaders can move around the room and pray individually with children. Keep encouraging all the children to pray out loud.

Tips:

- This is also a good time to pray for children who would like to receive Jesus as their Savior. Remind the children of the dirty glass and ask anyone who would like to have their hearts cleaned from sin to stand so that you can pray for them.

- When a child is filled with the Spirit, encourage him to keep praying out loud as an example to others. If you have time, you may have them share their experience in order to encourage other children. This may not be possible right away. If it is not, during your next class would be a good time to have children share their testimonies of being baptized in the Holy Spirit and of speaking in tongues.

- Be encouraging to all the children. Even if every child does not speak in tongues, remind them that they are being filled. Encourage them to keep asking God for His power; eventually they will be filled. Tell them that being filled doesn't have to happen only at church. It will happen when the Holy Spirit sees that their hearts are ready, and that they are ready to use His power to be witnesses.

OTHER RESOURCES

Boyd, Rev. David. "The Holy Spirit and Children," *Fanning the Flame*. The General Council of the Assemblies of God, Children's Ministries Agency, 20, (Spring 2006): 1-2.

Bridges, Rev. James K. "The Baptism in the Holy Spirit," *Fanning the Flame*. The General Council of the Assemblies of God, Children's Ministries Agency, 20, (Spring 2006): 6.

Burns, Rev. Billy. "Alive and Well in Your Kids," *Fanning the Flame*. The General Council of the Assemblies of God, Children's Ministries Agency, 20, (Spring 2006): 8.

Corbin, Rev. Ed & Sonja. "Leading Children in the Baptism in the Holy Spirit," *Children's Ministry Practicum*. Jackson's Ridge, South Africa, http://jacksonsridge.org (accessed March 12, 2007).

Crabtree, Rev. Charles. "The Holy Spirit in Me," *Fanning the Flame*. The General Council of the Assemblies of God, Children's Ministries Agency, 20 (Spring 2006): 12-13.

Elder, Rev. Keith. "Questions Children Ask about the Baptism in the Holy Spirit." http://4kids.ag.org/library/holy-spirit/index.cfm (accessed September 9, 2006).

The General Council of the Assemblies of God. *Statement of Sixteen Fundamental Truths*. Springfield, MO: Gospel Publishing House, 1994.

Gruber, Rev. Dick. "Baptism Basics." http://4kids.ag.org/library/holy-spirit/index.cfm (accessed September 9, 2006).

_____. "The Importance of the Altar." http://4kids.ag.org/library/holy-spirit/index.cfm (accessed September 9, 2006).

"The Holy Spirit and You." http://4kids.ag.org/library/holy-spirit/index.cfm (accessed September 9, 2006).

Horton, Rev. Stanley M, Th.D. "Your Sons and Your Daughters Will Prophesy." http://4kids.ag.org/library/holy-spirit/index.cfm (accessed September 9, 2006).

Jorris, Rev. Barry. "After the Altar: Keeping the Fire Burning after Kid's Camp," *Fanning the Flame.* The General Council of the Assemblies of God, Children's Ministries Agency, 20, (Spring 2006): 7.

Martin, Rev. Ray. "Leading Your Kids Into the Fullness of the Holy Spirit," *Fanning the Flame.* The General Council of the Assemblies of God, Children's Ministries Agency, 20, (Spring 2006): 9.

Mastrorio, Rev. Lorraine. "Helping a Child Receive the Baptism in the Holy Spirit." http://4kids.ag.org/library/holy-spirit/index.cfm (accessed September 9, 2006).

Rogge, Rev. Natalie. "Helping Kids Understand the Baptism in the Holy Spirit." http://4kids.ag.org/library/holy-spirit/index.cfm (accessed September 9, 2006).

"Teaching Pentecostal Distinctives to Children." http://4kids.ag.org/library/holy-spirit/index.cfm (accessed September 9, 2006).

OTHER DECADE OF PENTECOST PUBLICATIONS

Order from ActsinAfrica.org

Proclaiming Pentecost: 100 Sermons Outlines on the Power of the Holy Spirit (2011). Mark Turney and Denzil R. Miller, editors. (Also available in French, Spanish, Portuguese, and Swahili)

Globalizing Pentecostal Missions in Africa (2011). Denzil R. Miller and Enson Lwesya, editors. (Also available in French, 2014)

Power for Mission: The Africa Assemblies of God Mobilizing the Reach the Nations (2014). Denzil R. Miller and Enson Lwesya, editors.

From Azusa to Africa to the Nations: 2nd Edition (2014). Denzil R. Miller

AIA
PUBLICATIONS

POWER-FILLED!
Leading Children into the Baptism
into the Holy Spirit
by Philip Malcolm and Robin Malcolm
A Decade of Pentecost Publication
20147

www.ingramcontent.com/pod-product-compliance
Lightning Source LLC
Chambersburg PA
CBHW060139050426
42448CB00010B/2211